YOUR KNOWLEDGE HAS VALUE

- We will publish your bachelor's and master's thesis, essays and papers

- Your own eBook and book - sold worldwide in all relevant shops

- Earn money with each sale

Upload your text at www.GRIN.com
and publish for free

Bibliographic information published by the German National Library:

The German National Library lists this publication in the National Bibliography; detailed bibliographic data are available on the Internet at http://dnb.dnb.de .

Imprint:

Copyright © 2017 GRIN Verlag, Open Publishing GmbH
Print and binding: Books on Demand GmbH, Norderstedt Germany
ISBN: 9783668511972

This book at GRIN:

http://www.grin.com/en/e-book/374152/geographies-of-dispossession-to-bhoodan-repossession-climate-displacements

Sonali Narang

Geographies of Dispossession to "Bhoodan" Repossession-Climate Displacements

GRIN Publishing

GRIN - Your knowledge has value

Since its foundation in 1998, GRIN has specialized in publishing academic texts by students, college teachers and other academics as e-book and printed book. The website www.grin.com is an ideal platform for presenting term papers, final papers, scientific essays, dissertations and specialist books.

Visit us on the internet:

http://www.grin.com/

http://www.facebook.com/grincom

http://www.twitter.com/grin_com

Geographies of Dispossession to 'Bhoodan' Repossession-Climate Displacements

Dr. Sonali Narang, Lecturer, Department of Social Science, Panipat Institute of Engineering & Technology, Panipat, India.

Abstract

The impact of Forced displacement in South Asia will lead to scarcity and dispossession of land and create 'spaces of exception' and 'spaces of exclusion'. Such dispossession will create new 'global souls' [climate Refugees] and new social-cultural geographies of identity determined and organised on the basic of catastrophic climatic events. The momentous rejoinder to climate change will require sacrifices, strong regional Institutions with accurate governance and cooperation across multiple scales. Hitherto, the land management policies of the State in South Asia have failed in supporting the commons and the livelihoods options of the citizens and non-citizens alike. With emerging discourse of climate change new land management policies are indispensable that will further demand committed leadership and powerful regulation. The goal of this paper is to analyses the relevance of Bhoodan movement as an institution to govern the common property management and the use of natural resources in a sustainable way. This paper will further look into how this concept can be used inter-state or intra-state within South Asia towards climate displaced community across multiple logics of dispossession, violence and insecurity and where wider socio-economic, political and legal struggles come together and understand that whether it would be able to provide land and dignity to millions who will be crossing edge in search of protected lands and livelihood.

Keywords: South Asia, Climate Change, Bhoondan Movement, Climate displacements.

Introduction

The relationship between Climate Change to geography of 'dispossession' to geography of 'repossession' of land are multifaceted. The impacts of climate change on land is visible throughout the region of South Asia and these abrupt changes will be deteriorating accessibility of land for both productive use and resettlement of Climate displaced migrants. As a result, to scrutiny 'Bhoodan movement' as an option of reconsideration planning in order to secure future of environmental or climate migrants and by making arrangements for their resettlement either inter-state or intra-state within South Asia demands and deserves serious and systematic attention and further research. This paper offers new insights into the relationships between climate changes, geographies of dispossession and Bhoodan movement by integrating three disparate but well-founded bodies of research on the vulnerability of South Asian coastal regions particularly India and Bangladesh and examines the role of state in addressing the issue of climate displacements. Movement of Bhoodan will be anchored around issues of scarcities, survival, identity and reorganization.

Dispossession of climate geographies

Complex geography has been associated with Climate change both in terms of causes and consequences. Coastline sizeable coastal communities and ecosystems are highly vulnerable to changing climate. South Asia will be among those regions hardest hit by climate change. Higher temperatures, more extreme weather, rising sea levels, increasing cyclonic activity in the Bay of Bengal and the Arabian Sea, as well as floods in the region's complex river systems will complicate existing development and poverty reduction initiatives. Due to high population density levels, along with climate shifts will create complex environmental, humanitarian, and security challenges. India and Bangladesh, in particular, will feel the impacts of climate change intensely along with other development challenges. Extreme events and deteriorating conditions are likely to force many to leave their homes temporarily or even permanently for another village, city, region or country. The impacts of climate warming can be expected to have a range of direct impacts on land use systems, with both direct and indirect repercussions for land rights and access. Shifts in Climatic regions, rising sea levels and increases in extreme climatic events are likely to reduce the availability of land suitable for human settlement and agricultural production, as a result of temperature increases, marine level rise and associated flooding, and restrictions in water supply, leading to population migration and displacement and the need to adjust livelihood patterns to new circumstances. These changes will increase struggle for land and are likely to trigger changes in access to land and land tenure arrangements[i]. Many Climate Experts warn that climate change will increase resource conflicts within and among countries, increase migration pressures on hundreds of millions of people, disrupt economies all over the world, and threaten military preparedness[ii]. The areas where there is already existing conflict in South Asia, climate change is adding as stressor and changing existing migration patterns[iii]. It is imperative to begin examining the emerging climate confrontations to avoid future complex crisis scenarios. In Bangladesh, the capital Dhaka, currently a city of 13 million people, already suffers serious water-logging and drainage problems during the monsoon season. Climate Change will affect Dhaka in two prime ways: through floods and overstretched drainage systems, and through heat stress. Temperature rises in the Himalayas causing the melting of glaciers and snowfields, together with increased precipitation will lead to more frequent flooding, compounding the effects of sea level rise and more intense and frequent storm events[iv]. As a result of these changes, climate change could slow down the achievement of the Millennium Development Goals including those on poverty eradication, child mortality, malaria, and other diseases, and environmental sustainability. In addition, the impacts of climate change will exacerbate existing social and environmental problems and lead to migration within and across national borders. There has been some assumption that climate change may increase the risk of violent conflict[v]. The troubles, priorities and perspectives of forced migration appear to relatively ignore within South Asia particularly in India and Bangladesh. Forced displacements have been taking place at a colossal scale with consequences affecting spaces and societies beyond national borders and Bhoodan movement is a technique for local repossession of land either through the medium of interstate or intra state; a point to which we shall return shortly in the section to follow.

Role of the State and Climate displacements

The twenty first century will be witnessing endless flow of refugees and the developing states will bear the consequences. According to neo-Malthusian perspective climate change will be reducing resource base of vulnerable areas and there would be surplus population displaced by climate warming and that will lead to waves of climate refugees as matter of concern, it will further lead to destabilizing effects[vi]. There would be rivalry related to resources, scare resources become scarcer, injustice grow deeper, new social tensions give rise to violent conflict, civil war, and massive refugee flows. Climate change will pose new challenges in terms of resources, responsibility and justice[vii]. Increasing urbanisation and migration to coastal areas is already being experienced by Asia along with more frequent intense cyclones and storm surges already highly vulnerable to flooding, with much of the poorer urban population in coastal South and Southeast Asia housed in large extra-legal settlements[viii]. As pointed out by David Ludden (2004)[ix] in his intriguing piece of writing titled *India and South Asia: A short history* insightfully argues, in order to understand history inside South Asia, we must escape the confines of modern boundaries that enclose and separate civilizations to explore a wider world within which these boundaries have been invented, contested defended, and redrawn historically, it is therefore most appropriate to study South Asia as a huge open geographical space in southern Eurasia, rather than imagining it to be fixed historical region with a single territorial definition. Many scholars and climate experts estimated that people will suffer from landlessness in South Asia and particularly in the underdevelopment and poor regions of Bangladesh and India. Under the present circumstances, Bangladeshis are constructing their homes on boats and conducting classes for children over boats whose lands and property were flooded.

Despite land reform, land distribution has become unequal in recent years. Under the law, land holdings of former feudal landlords and private land holding above certain ceilings are intended to become public land known as 'khas land' intended for redistribution to the poor and landless. In practice however khas land is subject to extensive land grabbing by rural elites and former landlords, often closely associated with the political class and have social connections with [Climate] bureaucrats, political leaders and the judiciary, and forcible land occupation[x]. In view of the scale of the threats of displacement due to coastal and riparian flooding, migration would be inevitable and there may be a need to develop regional migration and adaptation programmes, including cooperation in resettlement policy[xi]. Climate-induced displacement puts more emphasis on the positive obligations of states to look forward and take measures to prevent or diminish conditions that may bring about dislocation. Many recent studies on the impact of climate change have predicted that even more people are likely to be displaced by the 2050 period [xii]and according to Professor Norman Myers (2005)[xiii] of Oxford University 200 million people would be displaced by 2050. He has further argued that the displaced people will have no other option but to seek asylum in another places despite all kinds of risks involved[xiv]. Both the Stern Committee review on the economics of Climate Change (2006)[xv] and a Christian Aid Report (2007)[xvi] have estimated displacement of 200 million and 250 million people respectively by climate change related phenomena. The Christian Aid Report entitled *"Human Tide: The Real Migration Crisis"* (2007) has predicted that almost one billion people will be displaced from

4

their homes between now and 2050. The report also points out that forced migration is the most urgent threat which the poor people will be facing in developing countries[xvii]. According to yet another major study titled *"In Search of Shelter: Mapping the Effects of Climate Change on Human Migration and Displacement"* (2009)[xviii] "the influence of environmental change on human mobility is visible and growing. Current and projected estimates vary widely, with figures ranging from 25 to 50 million by the year 2010 to almost 700 million by 2050"[xix] .The report endorses the International Organization for Migration (IOM) estimate of 200 million climate induced migrants by 2050. In the wake of 1 to 2 degree increase in temperature "About 85 per cent of the Maldives mainland which contains the capital Male, would be flooded. Most of the Maldives will be turned into sandbars, which will force 300,000 people to flee to India or Sri Lanka and even the country like Vietnam could lose 500,000 hectares of land in the Red River Delta and another 2 million hectares in the Mekong Delta, could displace near about 10 million people"[xx] .There is another view supported by Castles (Cited in Traufetter, 2007) the author of a well known book titled *"Age of Migration"* in which he argues that when living conditions do get intolerable, people are more likely to move within their own country rather than cross international borders. According to Castles we need more research on how people actually respond in a given area or region to environmental disaster, war, or widespread poverty. He has also given the example of the 1995 earthquake in Kobe, Japan, where most of the 300,000 displaced residents returned a few months later. After the Pinatubo volcano erupted in the Philippines, a large number of people returned to their respective homelands after some years. He also believes that the role of the government in mitigating the disasters is also important. The question then becomes: How well governments manage the things? States are critical to provide opportunities to displaced people, creating and providing a stable environment so that livelihoods can be pursued and take measures to provide protection and care. States in South Asia can exercise their sovereign rights to mediate between regional flows in ways that enhance and protect the certain group's livelihoods. 'The climate crisis that is likely to unfold in South Asia will create more profound challenges. With a 5-metre sea level rise, there will be about 125 million climate migrants in this region alone with little or no legal standing under current [National] and international law. In fact the 75 million or so from Bangladesh will be especially vulnerable, as their entire nation-state becomes non-viable as an entity, with most of its land inundated and its economy defunct'[xxi]. States can play critical roles in creating the conditions whereby people can act in ways to pursue the lives they value[xxii]. They can provide protective guarantees to assist people when their livelihoods suddenly contract, for example through income support, food aid, or short term local employment programs. They can provide social, economic and political freedoms. States are responsible to create provision for climate education and Climate care mechanism. States can provide transparency guarantees to ensure openness and accountability in transactions towards climate mitigate actions. These functions of States are interconnected, they "supplement" and "reinforce" each other[xxiii], and their instrumentality is maximised when all are in place. The geo-spacial and geo-cultural outcome of intra-state climate flows through resource induced micro movements will lead us to the thought of hybridity as an expression it is generally conceived of as a condition that transgresses or disconcerts binary geographies that are evoked to draw distinctions between like and unlike or self and other in the recent geographical transformation. In the case of post-colonial studies, the term has come to be 'associated with the interrogation of those contact spaces in which cultural differences are contingently and conflictally negotiated'[xxiv]. As a consequences of climate change, it evokes several geographies and not one; multiple geographical knowledge's produced at different places and for equally diverse purposes (ibid). Hybridity, according to Homi Bhabha (1999)[xxv] belongs to 'in between' spaces and can be captured in its various subtle nuances only through a counter history of South Asian identities, in which caste, creeds, religions ethnicities are seen as intervened in a multifaceted history of cosmopolitan hybrid of shared [climate] spaces. It is therefore critically important for the regional state and non-state actors of South Asia to reject the orthodox definition of 'Hybridity' and to think beyond their egocentric interests. Cultures of 'purity' will not arise without assimilating and understanding other's culture. As Michael Shapiro (1996:3)[xxvi] pointed out that the global system of sovereign states has been familiar with both structurally and symbolically in the daily acts of imaginations through which human space and identity are constructed. The persistence of this international imaginary has helped to support the political privilege of sovereignty affiliations and territorialities. The ultimate decision-maker is the state that calculates the loss of land dispossession and responsible to accommodate displaced people due to climatic reasons. 'The fact is that state is not the owner of natural resources. The state can at best be the custodian of natural resources that belong to people. The state as an institution in its self accountable to the nation and to its people' [xxvii]. Within South Asia, Bangladesh, India, and many small island states such as the Maldives face having to relocate large populations over the next 50 years as sea levels rise up to one metre. This would have profound effects on the 1.5 billion people who presently live in coastal areas. It is pointed out by Elizabeth Ferris (2012)[xxviii] that State Governments should be encouraging to establish land funds and to provide support to civil society. She

6

further eloquently stated that 'Governments are generally required to secure land for the resettlement of affected communities. But in practice, government authorities often declare that substitute land is unavailable, and resort to compensation rather than resettlement. This transfers the burden of finding land onto the shoulders of the displaced people themselves. In the case of climate related displacement, there are likely to be particular difficulties in finding suitable land for resettlement of communities from areas rendered uninhabitable because of the effects of climate change. Firstly, there simply may not be sufficient land available, for example, in Asian megadeltas where potentially millions of people may need to be resettled because of rising sea levels. Secondly, there is likely to be increased pressure on the availability of suitable land for resettlement sites. Thus, if fishing communities need to be resettled because of the erosion of coastlines and sea level rise due to climate change, it is unlikely that it would be easy to find alternatives sites for them- at least in coastal areas which would enable them to continue their traditional livelihoods. Similarly, if large areas of a country are deemed unsuitable for habitation because of drought, the overall availability to land is likely to drastically diminish and land will become much more expensive'[xxix]. Walter Kalin, the former Representative of the Secretary General on Human Rights of Internally Displaced Persons and now head of the Nansen Initiative emphasised that a person who cannot be reasonably expected to return his/her place of habitual residence should be considered a victim of forced displacement and be granted at the very least a temporary stay within safe third countries[xxx]. Expert like Scot Leckie (2014)[xxxi] have proposed an alternative before receiving state to provide rights to climate displaced persons as enjoyed by refugees and to the maximum extent like the citizens of the country concerned. Under human rights law, climate displaced persons are those who are forced by circumstances beyond their control to move across an international border 'are to be entered general human rights guarantees in the receiving state, but do not generally possess right to enter that state'[xxxii]. In the absence of state climate laws the condition of climate displaced community will be further deteriorating and uncertain.

Climate induced assimilation – The Battle for land and [Law] in South Asian Region

Most of the South Asian countries are not the signatory of the 1951 UN convention of refugee came into existence against the backdrop of the Second World War; they call international refugee law as "alien to their needs, interests and experiences"[xxxiii]. Asian countries were not given adequate participation in the drafting of these laws. When it comes to refugee, this has led to a lawless situation in South Asia. To quote Aung Phyro and Tapan

Bose (2009:148) 'the postcolonial states in South Asia were born out of displacement and expulsion of a large number of people and the state system, as it stands today in the region, is perched precariously in the creation of minorities, stateless population and the continuing exodus of victims of various conditions. There are no national laws, which define and regulate the status of the refugee in the countries of South Asia'[xxxiv]. The notion of Assimilation are based upon mappings of the world outside one's border and should be interpreted in part as a geopolitical discourse through which political actors make sense of 'our place' in a wider system of political, cultural and territorial entities[xxxv]. Political geographer like C.R Nagel (2002) to question assumptions about both assimilation and non-assimilation found in the literature on transnationalism. According to Nagel: 'In focusing the debate on whether transnationalism is new or old and whether immigrants assimilate or do not assimilate, we neglect to explain the complex negotiations of power and identity implicated in the definition of social membership and assimilability across historical and geographical contexts... explaining the dynamics of immigrants inclusion and exclusion does not require a 'new' theory of transnationalism as much it requires an understanding of the geopolitical[climate change] practices and discourses that underpin the regulation of human mobility'[xxxvi](ibid:224). Land policies are debated widely and presenting opportunities to ensure that land policies are adequately "climate proofed" as part of the reform process, so as to anticipate the future demands of climate change. The likely requirements for resettlement of displaced people and relocation in cropping systems, government land acquisition, improved land use regulation and environmental protection as part of national adaptation strategies mean that land policy itself needs to be clearly mainstreamed within national planning and adaptive frameworks[xxxvii]. Geography is not only an economic asset for rural people but it comprises dignity for them but due to adverse impacts of climate change which leads to dispossession, affecting marginalized, tribal, indigenous community, women and children most dramatically in absence of programme strong movements and organizations to compensate that may benefit the rural poor. The increasing landlessness as a result of sudden disasters has being witnessing by the developing countries of Global South. Many countries from developing regions such as Bangladesh, Maldives and Tuvalu are already in a process of buying land and planning to move their people to safer places like Sri Lanka, India, England New Zealand and Australia. Bangladesh has to deal with millions of people who are likely to be displaced in the next few years. When the time comes countries of South Asia left with no choice but to manage the risk of mass migration. Bangladesh leaders and climate specialists strongly believe that richer nations should accept climate refugees from

Bangladesh. A useful example of counter-geographies is from Mr Abdul Maal Abdul Muhith, the finance minister in the COP15 emphatically pointed out the moral responsibility of Britain, the USA and other countries of global north to accept climate refugees of Bangladesh by stating that 'UK should open borders to climate refugees'. Prior to the Copenhagen Climate Summit, the Finance Minister stated that: "We are asking all our development partners to honour the natural right of persons to migrate. We can't accommodate all these people – this is already the densest [populated] country in the world."[xxxviii]. At the 64th Session of the United Nations General Assembly, on 26 September 2009, Sheikh Hasina, the Prime Minister of Bangladesh, while expressing her concern about implications of climate change for her country, talked in the same breath about millions of ' climate migrants' and 'climate refugees' and need for an international legal regime. Around the same time the 'Bangladesh Climate Change Strategy and Action Plan 2009' was released. In her message to the Action Plan, Prime Minister Sheikh Hasina expressed the resolve of her government to 'free' the people of her country from the "terror of climate" and to ensure that "people are fully protected from its adverse impacts as promised in our manifesto"[xxxix]. It has been estimated that there is the impending threat of displacement of more than 20 million people in the event of sea-level change and resulting increase in salinity coupled with impact of increase in cyclones and storm surges, in the near future. The settlement of these environmental refugees will pose a serious problem for the densely populated Bangladesh and migration must be considered as a valid option for the country. Preparations in the meantime will be made to convert this population into trained and useful citizens for any country[xl]. In Maldives too one finds a broad spectrum of imaginative geographies and narratives revolving around Climate induced displacement and migrations. Maldivian President Mohamed Nasheed stated that the country, with a population of over 396,000, also had plans to buy a new homeland overseas as an insurance policy against climate change. Nasheed apparently assured: We do not want to leave the Maldives, but we also do not want to be climate refugees living in tents for decades. Sri Lanka and India are our targets because they have similar cultures, cuisines and climates. Australia is also being considered because of the amount of unoccupied land available. The country's government held the world's first Cabinet meeting underwater to highlight the danger faced by global warming. He said that "We have not decided on the financial aspects of the deal. However, Maldives should pay the minimal amount. Meanwhile, we don't think that this dredging is going to have any impact on the Bangladesh environment"[xli]. It is difficult to overlook underlying fear and anxieties in the tone and the tenor of State's actor in their discourses of climate change. States, people,

9

community those who will be losing land, will be required it for new settlements either internally or beyond a nation's borders when national land resources are no longer viable. The conclusion of the Pacific Consultation of the Nansen Initiative held in May 2013 importantly recognized the following imperative: Take measures such as land audits, demarcation of uncontested boundaries and community land mapping to facilitate the identification of land when people need to be temporarily or permanently moved, within their own country or abroad', and that at the international level steps should be taken to 'Encourage discussions regarding resources being made available within the framework of existing or new international financial mechanisms to cover costs and investments related to displacement and planned relocation, and to compensate for loss of community ties, land, and cultural assets[xlii]. In this paper, we are in a process of understanding Bhoodan movement in order to reduce land based challenges that climate displaced community is likely to experience due to environmental degradation and who are looking towards new land resources within South Asia. There is need for South Asian protocol and climate cooperation on climate related movements. The global geographies of dispossession due to environmental factors that formed the back-story to revisit Bhoodhan Movement with in South Asia lead towards geography of repossession in the region.

Governing of Climate displacements: The Bhoodan Way

The Twenty first century will be witnessing numerous micro and regional geopolitical movements for the protection of land rights for displaced climate community by using local spaces either inter-state or across borders. A Social movement emerges to meet a 'newly-felt need'[xliii]. Blumer (1951) too argues that social movements arise out of 'undefined or unstructured situations' which cause stresses in the system. Geo- spacial-cultural movements either inter or intra state means a set of social- spatial strategies of resistance adopted by communities on the margins against the dominant narratives (understanding) and written geographies of meaning forcibly imposed on their respective rooted localities and livelihoods. What are unfolding in South Asia would be micro geo- spatial-cultural movements of resistance like Bhoodan movement for the land against the neo- liberal world order, International and National climate change discourses and Climate action plans of States that tend to push into unconsciousness the long standing histories of environmental injustices. There is considerable literature to show why landless people start movements and confrontation in order to attain land[xliv]. The movement of Bhoondan would start from local spaces then moving across regional spaces against every geographical scales of climate

10

problem from local to the global. This movement would be an attempt of repossession of geography through aid, donation and development assistance either within a country or if required then across the region. Bhoodan movement wanted the ownership of land to be broad, humane and flexible, but though there was some decentralisation in ownership patterns, it did not break through much[xlv]. The Bhoondan movement has been described as the result of decentralized and locally autonomous movements. The geo-historical meaning of Bhoodan denotes as land gift. When the role of State and Markets are failed to manage the resources in sustainable manner then the issue of Common Property Resources(CPRs) will be re-emerged into Global discussion and then the third alternative will be the role of institution to govern these resources. Bhoodan and Gramdan are such institutions, designed by Vinoba Bhave who was a practitioner and started this movement in India in the framework of common property management and used natural resources in a sustainable way. The philosophy of Bhoondan was that Vinoba Bhave appealed to big land owners to distribute their land as gift to landless poor. He called it Bhoodaan that gradually culminated into Gramdan, where the land of the entire village was donated to the community and treated as community property. Bhoodan was not only gift, but 'sharing together' according to Vinoba bhave while "Gramdan was equitable sharing together of the lands of the village by the people of the village" and thus Bhoodan signified distribution of land to the landless, Gramdan, on the other hand, meant communisation of the land: institution of community, in place of individual ownership of land[xlvi]. Thus 'the idea of Bhoodan became a total agrarian revolution, a beautiful and different type of revolution, without force or compulsion but on the basis of mutual surrender to the community. 'The outward social change was accompanied by inward human change'[xlvii]. It was on Bhoodan activity and soon became a movement in whole of India. About 4 million acres or 1.6 million hectare of land was received as daan – gift till 1970, when the activity ended. The land distributed to landless 16 had inheritance rights but did not give right to alienate. Bhoodaan is a case of collective ownership and private use[xlviii]. Bhoodan, and subsequently Gramdan, were methods of collecting land through private initiatives in India [South Asia Region] for distribution among the landless agricultural labourers in our case [climate induced displaced/ migrants]. This was a response to the radical peasant riots in Telengana region in Andhra Pradesh in India and went parallel to the non-legitimized path like 'Land Grab' practiced by the political radicals in India since early independence [xlix]. The displacement by climate change not only destroys the socio-economic and cultural fabric of society but the inherited skills or indigenous knowledge of the people and intergenerational social relations that have shaped over

11

generations. As a result, the entire world is under the threat of environmental degradation struggle. Many cultural geographers, academics and intellectuals of the world have been contemplating on this issue and realized to the extent that there should be change from below pointing beyond the existing system in support of new geography of transformation. Like The Ruskin's book 'Unto This Last', this indicates that even the last person should get an equivalent share. The Russian author Tolstoy wrote a story on land. In this story, he raised the question of how much land does a man need, after all? In the beginning of the 20th century, Madhavrao Sapre wrote a story titled '*Ek tokri bhar mitti*' and Hindi movie titled *Do Bigha Zamin* ("two-thirds of an acre of land) in 1953 which depicted the issue of forceful land occupation by Zamindars to our concern here land is like to be occupied by climatic effects. On similar themes, stories titled '*Garib ki Haaye*' and '*Balidaan*' were penned by eminent Hindi writer, Premchand[l]. The Movement attracted the attention of many thinkers from outside India too. Like Louis Fischer, the famous American Correspondent expressively stated that 'Gramdan is the most creative thought coming from the East in recent times'. The American Ambassador to India, Chester Bowles in his seminal work insightfully argues that: *The Dimensions of Peace* expressed that in 1955 the Bhoodan Movement was giving the message of Renaissance in India. It offered a revolutionary alternative to communism, as it was founded on human dignity. The British industrialist, Earnest Barder was deeply impressed by the Bhoodan Movement and implemented the Gandhian concept of Trusteeship by allocating 90 percent share in the company to his industrial workers. The space of dispossession is being created by climate crises and place of repossession will be created by Bhoodan movement. Prof. Tinbergin aptly stated that "the rich of the earth should prepare themselves for the simple life in future. The leading philosophy of the present day society which always asks for more material goods and does not attach much value at simplicity of life, or modesty in claims has to be replaced by alternative philosophies and surely could be learned from Mahatma Gandhi's words and examples. The real values of life do contain a sufficient quality of goods and shelter, but it is not necessary to have luxuries now aimed at. Cultural Values will have to be upgraded now"[li]. Bhoodan movement is a private institutional attempt to resettle those people who will be forced to move due to climatic factors either within their own region or across borders. It was on that 1951, Bhoodan Movement started for bringing out reforms in Land within India. But in this paper we are using this movement for land rights of climate migrants and displace community through Institutional method of Bhoodan that seems to be relevant in context of South Asia. The first Bhoodan (land-gift) of hundred acres was made on April 18, 1951 to Vinoba Bhave, the initiator of the movement.

Later the donations widened out into Gramdan, donation of entire villages. It was on May 1952, the first Gramdan was made by the villagers of Mangrot in Hamirpur district of Uttar Pradesh. The Akhli Bharat Sarva Seva Sangh, Kashi, works as the coordinating agency of the Sarva Seva Sanghs established on a State-wise basis. The crucial role also played by magazines and Journals started appearing like *Bhoodan Yajna* (in Hindi) started in 1954. Since 1956 *'Bhoodan'* is being published in English. Both these publications are weeklies and are edited by Dhirendra Muzumdar. Gramdan, started in 1957 and edited by A W Sahasrabudhe and Sachidanand. These publications are exclusively devoted to reporting the progress of the Bhoodan and Gramdan movement; but publication like Sarvodaya and Gandhi Marg too publicise the activities of the movement[lii].

Conclusions

Micro geo-spacial cultural movement like Bhoodan are expected to meet social needs of migrants and create new social-cultural relationships and collaborations both within national and across geographical scale and against all socio-political hierarchies. The countries of South Asia should start this movement in order to accommodate displaced climate migrants within their country or across boundaries which further needs strong institutional leadership. The major intention of this paper is to argue that the issue of climate induced displacements and migrations within South Asia can be better approached and analysed as a process and could be grip through the Bhoodan movement. Despite many post-colonial constrains to address the problem of climate displacements but the basic aspects could be resolved through movement of Bhoodan in South Asia region with land based solutions. Despite all the limitation of ordering, bordering and othering of Westphalian state system Bhoondan Movement would ever be deemed as magnificent attempt for a non-violent solution of the basic land problem of the coastal regions and underdeveloped regions of South Asia continent. Climate change can be viewed as opportunity for a non-violent reconstruction and transformation of society towards Climate induced egalitarian society that emphasizes equal treatment of climate induced migrants within their own region or across borders, irrespective of gender, religion, economic status and ideologies and beliefs. Acharya Vinoba opined that everyone had a right to land. He believed in a phrase that all the land belongs to Him (God). In order to make this movement successful, South Asia needs to rise above from the moral-scared geography of otherness and acknowledge the long-standing patterns of cultural intermingling and geographies of peaceful coexistence and solidarity. We could think of shared spaces of different sub-category of climate migrants and truly cosmopolitan place

13

where cultures of climate migrants are celebrated not only for their fusion of differences across borders but also for coming together the combination of different forms of belief or practices.

Endnotes

[i] Quan Julian and Nat Dyer.(2008). "Climate Change and Land Tenure The Implications of Climate Change for Land Tenure and Land Policy". *IIED (International Institute for Environment and Development) and Natural Resources Institute* (2008). Accessed January 1, 2017 ftp://ftp.fao.org/docrep/fao/011/aj332e/aj332e00.pdf

[ii] Bhattacharyya Arpita and Werz Michael. "Climate Change, Migration, and Conflict in South Asia: Rising Tensions and Policy Options Across the Subcontinent". Washington: Center for American Progress. (2012). Accessed January 1, 2017. https://www.americanprogress.org/issues/security/reports/2012/12/03/46382/climate-change-migration-and-conflict-in-south-asia/

[iii] (ibid)

[iv] NEF and IIED. (2005a). "Up in smoke? Asia and Pacific The threat from climate change to human development and the environment". The fifth report from the Working Group on Climate Change and Development, *IIED*, London. Accessed June 28, 2016 http://www.iied.org/pubs/pdfs/10020IIED.pdf.

[v] Homer-Dixon. T."On the threshold: environmental changes as causes of acute conflict". *International Security*", 16(1991): 76-116.
Van. I, Klaassen.et.al . Climate change: Socioeconomic impacts and violent conflict. Dutch National Research Programme on Global Air Pollution and Climate Change"(1996) Report No. 410 200 006, Wageningen.
[vi] Hartmann, B. "Strategic Security: The origin and impacts of Environmental conflict ideas". PhD diss., Development Studies Institute, London School of Economics and Political Science, (2003).

[vii] Welzer, Harald. *Climate Wars: What People Will Be Killed For in the 21st Century*. Cambridge: Polity, 2012.

[viii] McGranahan, Gordon , Deborah, Balk and Anderson, Bridget. "The rising tide: assessing the risks of climate change and human settlements in low-elevation coastal zones". *Environment and Urbanization* 19(2007): 17–37. Accessed November 29 2016 .http://www.iied.org/HS/documents/eu19.pdf.

[ix] Ludden. David. (2004). *India and South Asia: A short History*. Oxford: One World Publication: 15-16, 2007.

[x] Barkat, Abul, Zaman uz Shafique, Raihan. Selim. *The Political Economy of Khas land in Bangladesh*. Association for Land Reform and Development: Dhaka, 2001.

[xi] (NEF & IIED 2005a)

[xii] Chowdhury, Afsan. "The coming Crisis: from Bangladesh to India . . . & then the rest". *Himal South Asian*, October. 2009

[xiii] Myers, Norman. "Environmental Refugees: An Emergent Security Issue". Paper presented at the 13th Economic Forum, Prague, May 23-27, 2005.

[xiv] Norman Myers, 2005.

[xv] Stern, Nicholas Herbert .*The economics of climate change: the Stern review*. Cambridge, UK: Cambridge University Press, 2007.

[xvi] Christian Aid. (2007). Human Tide: The Real Migration Crisis-A Christian Aid Report. London: Christian Aid.

[xvii] ibid

[xviii] Warner, K.; Erhart, C.; Sherbinin, A. de; Adamo, S. In search of shelter: mapping the effects of climate change on human migration and displacement, (2009), http://www.ciesin.columbia.edu/documents/clim-migr-report-june09_media.pdf

[xix] (Ibid: 21).

[xx] (Chowdhury, Afsan, 2009:4).

[xxi] Byravan, Sujatha and Rajan, Sudhir Chella. "The Social Impacts of Climate Change in South Asia", (2008). Accessed February 28 2016 https://ssrn.com/abstract=1129346 or http://dx.doi.org/10.2139/ssrn.1129346.

[xxii] Sen. A. (1999). Development as freedom. New York: Anchor Books. Shapiro. M.(1996). Introduction to Part 1, in Michael Shapiro and Hayward Alker (Eds.), Challenging Boundaries(pp.30). Minneapolis, MN: University of Minneaspolis Press. Shahi, V. (2011). From Bhoodan to an Alternative Development Model. Anasakti Darshan, 5(2) : 6(1).

[xxiii] (Sen 1999: 40)

[xxiv] Whatmore, Sarah. " Hybridity". In The Dictionary of Human Geography edited by Gregory.D, Johnston. R, Pratt.G, Watts. M.J & Whatmore. S. (pp, 361). Fifth edition, Oxford: Wiley-Blackwell, 2009.

[xxv] Bhabha, Homi. "The Location of culture". London: Routledge, 1991.

[xxvi] Shapiro. M. "Introduction to Part 1". In Challenging Boundaries edited by Michael Shapiro and Hayward Alker (pp.30). Minneapolis, MN: University of Minneaspolis Press, 1996.

[xxvii] Majumder, Bhaskar. "Regional Development and Dispossession: Some Experiences on land Acquisition in India, Journal of Regional Development and Planning", 1(2), 103, 2012.

[xxviii] Ferris. E. (2012). Protection and Planned Relocations in the Context of Climate Change, Legal and Protection Policy Research Series, August, UNHCR/PPLA/2012/04.Geneva: Division of International Protection, UNHCR, 21.

[xxix] ibid

[xxx] Kalin. Walter. "Displacement caused by the Effects of Climate Change: Who will be Affected and what are the Gaps in the Normative Framework for their Protection?" .Background paper, 2008.

16

[xxxi] Leckie, Scot. Land Solutions for Climate Displacement, business and economics. London: Route ledge, 2014.

[xxxii] ibid

[xxxiii] Davies E, Sara ."The Asian Rejection? International Refugee Law in Asia". *Australian Journal of Politics and History*, 52(4), 2006.

[xxxiv] Aung Phyro and Tapan Bose. "Protection of Refugees, Migrants, Internally and Stateless Persons". *Refugee Watch Issue* No. 1, January 1998.

[xxxv] O Tuathail, Gerald. "Geopolitics and discourse: practical geopolitican reasoning in American foreign policy". *Political Geography*, 11(2):190-204, 1992.

[xxxvi] Nagel. Caroline. "Geopolitics by Another Name: Immigration and Politics of Assimilation". Political geography, 21(8): 971-87, 2002.

[xxxvii] (Quan & Dyer 2008)

[xxxviii] (The Daily Star, 2009)

[xxxix] Ministry of Environment and Forestry Government of Bangladesh. (2009). "Bangladesh Climate Change Strategy and Action Plan" 2009. Accessed May 2016 http://cmsdata.iucn.org/downloads/bangladesh_climate_change_strategy_and_action_pl an_2009.pdf.

[xl] (Government of Bangladesh 2009, 17; emphasis given)

[xli] Jacob. S. (2010). "Bangladesh sand to help keep the Maldives afloat". *Bussiness Standard*, Accessed 2 May 2015. http://www.business-standard.com/article/economy-policy/bangladesh-sand-to-help-keepthe-maldives-afloat-110122800001_1.html.

[xlii] (ibid)

[xliii] Davis, Joseph.*Contemporary Social Movements*. (New York: D Appleton Century Company, 1930).

[xliv] (wolf 1969, Migdal 1974; Paige 1975; Popkin 1976; Scott 1976; Jenkins 1982; Skocpol 1982; McClintock 1984; Linchbach 1994; Wood 2003; Mason 2004).

[xlv] Sahi, Vinod. "From Bhoodan to an Alternative Development Model". *Anasakti Darshan Bhoodan Special Issue.2011*, Accessed 7 December 2016 http://www.mkgandhi.org/vinoba/anasakti/vinodshahi.htm .

[xlvi] Narayan, Jaya. Prakash. (1964). "Socialism, Sarvodaya and Democracy" (Eds.) by Bimla Prasad,pp.161, (Asia Publishing House: Bombay).

[xlvii] Singh, Rajender. "Bhoodan Movement As A Noble Revolution: Jayaparakash Narayan", *International Indexed & Refereed Research Journal*, IV(46), 2013.

17

[xlviii] Shukla. N and Iyengar. S."Governing of Commons: The Bhoodan Way". Conference Paper at the Conference of the International Association for the Study of the Commons, 2011 Accessed 18th September 2014 http://dlc.dlib.indiana.edu/dlc/handle/10535/7285. .

[xlix] Nanekar, K.R. & Khandewale. S.V. "Bhoodan and the Landless". (Popular Prakashan: Bombay, 1973): 27-28, 2, 8.

[l] Manimala, M. "Log aate gaye aur karwan banta gaya". *Anasakti Darshan.* July and June, (2010 &2011) Accessed 1 May 2016 http://www.mkgandhi.org/ebks/anashakti_english.pdf .

[li] Sharma. Manish. *Non-violence in the 21st Century: Application and Efficacy.* (New Delhi: Deep and Deep Publications, 2006):153

[lii] Oommen, TK. "Problems of Gramdan A Study in Rajasthan". *The Economic weekly.* June 26, 1965. Accessed 2 December 2016
http://www.epw.in/system/files/pdf/1965_17/26/problems_of_gramdana_study_in_rajasthan.pdf

YOUR KNOWLEDGE HAS VALUE

- We will publish your bachelor's and master's thesis, essays and papers

- Your own eBook and book - sold worldwide in all relevant shops

- Earn money with each sale

Upload your text at www.GRIN.com
and publish for free